T0046527

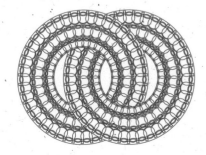

MAUSOLEUM OF FLOWERS

MAUSOLEUM
OF FLOWERS

DANIEL B. SUMMERHILL

CavanKerry
PRESS

CavanKerry Press Ltd.
Fort Lee, New Jersey
www.cavankerrypress.org

Publisher's Cataloging-In-Publication Data
(Prepared by The Donohue Group, Inc.)
Names: Summerhill, Daniel B., author.
Title: Mausoleum of flowers / Daniel B. Summerhill.
Description: First edition. | Fort Lee, New Jersey : CavanKerry Press, 2022.
Identifiers: ISBN 9781933880914
Subjects: LCSH: African Americans—Social life and customs—Poetry. | Loss
    (Psychology)—Poetry. | Spirituality—Poetry. | Family—Poetry. | LCGFT: Poetry.
Classification: LCC PS3619.U45938 M38 2022 | DDC 811/.6—dc23

Cover photo by Julie Meme/Stocksy United
Cover and interior text design by Ryan Scheife, Mayfly Design
First Edition 2022, Printed in the United States of America

CAVANKERRY
PRESS

Made possible by funds from the
New Jersey State Council on the Arts, a partner
agency of the National Endowment for the Arts.

CavanKerry Press is grateful for the support it receives from the
New Jersey State Council on the Arts.

In addition, CavanKerry Press gratefully acknowledges generous
emergency support received during the COVID-19 pandemic from
the following funders:

Community of Literary Magazines and Presses
New Jersey Arts and Culture Recovery Fund
New Jersey Council for the Humanities
New Jersey Economic Development Authority
Northern New Jersey Community Foundation
The Poetry Foundation
US Small Business Administration

Also by Daniel B. Summerhill

Divine, Divine, Divine (2021)

for Genesis

do not speak to me of martyrdom
of men who die to be remembered
on some parish day.
i don't believe in dying
though i too shall die
and violets like castanets
will echo me.

—Sonia Sanchez

It ain't perfect, but everything's beautiful here

—Jhené Aiko

CONTENTS

do not gather flowers for me,

yet
a black cadillac first, a hundred—
a buick will do if old enough
it's all about the body
& what it's borne anyway
line them up—out front
then,
let the chrysanthemums
roses & carnations
spill
out each window

make it magnificent

rev the engines—

until they are voiceless
until there is no gas
        left in the cylinders
until a mushroom cloud
of grey-black exhaust can be seen
from the heavens

anything this large
& dying
must have god's attention

wading

> *the water teaches:*
> *no one is special, no one is special*
> —Aracelis Girmay

i can't say i remember surviving

but do remember prolonged—

        drowning

the pool see-through &

blue

                like a city of glass

        my skin

my limbs: methodic & steady

bathing but not bathing—

                  wading

    mama's legs

        along the edge

unscattered

        there is a home here

quiet as a dead thing

              staying—

when we say it's in us, not on us

okay, so boom: we die but don't die, like hip hop or Tupac, but more serious like demigods playing spades / cutthroat / we bleed & flowers bloom where the drops land / american fruit / skin bruised / juicy / rich in vitamin a, b, c, d & endurance / got plenty of soul / call it the fight organ / it stays and stays like kin / our blood got fist / & if that don't make sense / consider this: you can't make gumbo without the roux

sunday in oakland

— you ask about the weather outside in an attempt to
stretch our visit & for the next 22 minutes flaxen leaves
smother the ground, the clouds are selfless & oakland
is golden today like all other days because oakland
measures its weather by the number of Black bodies
basking in the sun around lake merritt.

by now, the most complicated thing you can remember
of me is my name & how it forces your tongue to press
against the roof of your mouth twice before the tension
in your jaw is released. it is your only exercise. routinely,

you spend your time in bed until you don't, & then, like
a moment at *attention!* the day is as grand as your body will
allow. oxfords, where the creases excavate themselves into
a groove. a porkpie crown & a shirt that you ironed collar
first for the trip to refill your bag of chia seeds & other
items your va doctor recommended mostly aimed

at preservation of a body that broke in '43 during
the swing of the allies' fist. your power chair hoists a flag
that isn't red white & blue, but is as american as jim crow
& you and what's left of the 92nd infantry clasp onto your
buffalos as if they're the only thing you've claimed as
your own.

it's sunday. & if there was a day of the week to sink into
yourself, it would have to be the lord's day, no matter your
position to god. you are no exception to this rule. you sit
at the edge of a bed that is also half machine & ask me to
turn the tv down before, in a swift motion, you bring
your legs to rest on your mattress. their stiff landing,

the last thing i hear from you. & your breathing slows almost still. your nasal passages soften as if rehearsing how to leave gently & i'm reminded how some stars we admire don't exist anymore. how, by the time we praise them, they've already shrapneled into god's palms—

america is the only living thing that don't complain when the rain doesn't come

& i know, i savor death
       all too well,   bring her to my lips
let her rest   on my tongue
          run my fingers
     down her scarred body.
she is still,   a boulder in the wind
     tracing the corners
of her peaks back
       to my palms:
a black terrain. i grab a fistful,
     it fragments to my feet.
returning to my knees,   i tuck my chin
        to my chest
the best way i know how.

              this is the way
mama liberty   taught me   to worship
           to pray
to a country that died
       long before i had
arrived.

Enoch's second trip to earth

Black folks don't believe in free
the way it's spelled, but believe

in sowing seeds as wide as uh' mouth
full of blues, for brighter days, we say,

for later. we say. 365 years before
god plucked him from the earth

like an aster in a field of fire flowers.
perhaps, freedom isn't being plucked

from the earth like an aster, but
allowing our bones to decompose

underground, slowly. perhaps we sow
to escape the austerity of death

and find sovereignty in our rhythm.
a song and a seed are all that remains

when we die. maybe god wanted his
blues back. & Johnson wanted

to stay a while—this time. or
to decompose   at least.

"o" for *oh*

you pray & use "o"
as prefix to *god*

leave   "o"   dangling
                                        between
                                        your mouth &
                                        god's ear

leave

       interpretation
                as endearment
                as distance
                as plea

"o" for *oh*

"o" for interjection

           for oxygen

as in:

yo, god,

here i am   *gasping for air*

                          //

                     please

                          //

shoutin'

call stomping
the ground & flailing
               around
like an unwound
      windup: shoutin'

because the body is louder
than the mouth

for this reason, among others,
i forget
           to pray
at night

can't imagine any conversation
holier than the collarbone &
the quiet flesh attached to it

how it moves
           like a foot
in a mother's round belly
during the sixth month

      it too knows, somehow:

motion plus
           a body

equals deliverance

fear

after Kendrick Lamar

in the savanna, a calf watches
a matriarch heave
      an acacia branch
with her trunk
after moments earlier plucking
a blade of grass from the earth
& does not consider her body
a non sequitur

// //

i'll beat yo' ass is malleable

// //

what is a good metaphor
      for an elephant?

// //

thick palm wrecking a world
for a moment
then cleaning the wound
with rubbing alcohol & vaseline.

// //

milkweed & black-eyed susans
endure the winter

// //

i, too, am perennial

//

do not withhold discipline
from a child; if you punish them
with the rod, they will not die

//

i'll beat yo' ass:
embalming fluid
not a fear tactic

//

i'll beat yo' ass if
i beat yo' ass twice
      & you still here

//

o little black belt, you
make everything
more tangible. death
is no monster here,
but the goal. an elastic holy
grail sculpted over
an entire adolescence

//

**i used to believe there wasn't anything
a Black woman's prayer couldn't fix**

        i've argued *your* prayer
could fix anything
        until moments after watching Dre pulled
from his car

        having his body taken,
i realized there are two things
        knees & cupped hands
won't deliver me from:
        death &

        the blow of a baton

not to downplay breath
        but i understand
the connection between heaven & hell

        or the colonization of it

Frank's opus: poolside convo erasure

Frank Ocean shares notes about the making of blond *in boys don't cry magazine, 2016*

        years ago, i found   a cross swept,

     behind the road   myself   her

then played   all hits

     as the seat belt   tightens   pressing
     forward then

     backwards and forward again there i got free

and there's no practical reason

                       out here

but i guess it's good to have   in case of emergency   maybe

         i don't want my memories

close-by   casting at random   for the fuck of it

in conversation   i shed a tear   for my favorite part of
life

     i convince myself   though

                  it's still all good.

mama

knows what it's like to hold & not
   be held   Mama Nancy, who is not my
mama, but is the oldest mama i have

a name for   in this way, history is
   young, not because it is young, but
because it goes only as far back as

our stories do & i'd like to think
   memory counts for something   three
women separate her from my mama,

each of them a comma, each of them
   should have been a semicolon, but we
know genealogy isn't forgiving that

way   i'm the son of all four   & i am
   told, by Mama, that her earliest recall
of joy was being handed a quarter

to buy a hamburger & still having
   15 cents left over to buy penny
candy   this girl, a woman, a mother

who has never been to the bottom
   of the earth   & not that any long-haul
flight will buy happiness, but being

awakened by the unswallowed sun over
   the southern ocean seems like a cheat code
for sustained joy   i say sustained in

the sense that the sunrise is the only
   infinite rhythm i've seen   this isn't
a poem about joy, so much as it is

a poem about dying without ever knowing
   it   but Mama, you've always stricken me
as someone who champions distance over

depth   or faith over long suffering   in
   this way, i suppose joy isn't the antonym
to pain, but the antibody   it is 1998, &

you have just given me a pink
   food stamp, enough to buy a zebra cake,
kool-aid jammer, and three packs of now

and laters   the walk to the corner store:
   my faith, the slow skip back home: small
joy   here, my perception of small is grand

enough to get me through the immensity
   of summer   how my mother summoned
enough jubilance to share with me   its

blood   it is 2018 & i think of my trip to
   south africa as a metaphor for food stamps,
the flight: my faith; the flight: my joy—

what i don't deserve, not considered here
   the miles between me & the earth: stretched
faith   carrying me back home   i search

out my window for land, but find nothing
   green, just blue   plenty blue to feel small
enough to remember my small mama

with outstretched hands—waiting
   for a quarter, for joy   a girl, a woman, dear
Mama: your water will come, & the sun

will brass-knuckle its way out of the ocean
   with enough triumph to make you feel
golden   the ocean is the only constant

here, it delivers us all, i'd imagine
   it'll deliver you too, if not you, your body,
if not your joy, your pain, it will carry it

in its mouth, back to shore, like a flood

on deciding to leave my tail out

the only way to avoid the Hand of God is to get in it.
     —Toni Morrison, *Sula*

i pull the narrow flaps

behind each ear twice // a

half bow behind the medulla—

here is where it gets good //

this tail makes me feel

even more

Black,

which is

to say: *i feel*

even holier

with nylon

flailing

from

my neck

Frank's opus: nikes

is a collective belch—
the eyes too

      have a disgusting sound to them

swallowed a boy
whole

is bravado, tiny mating call, call it
      we want to fit—
      in a three-ring binder's cover slip
or prayer's lips or between lips

      we're both hungry this way

you split your eyes,
      i get the rogue one
& if one of us should fall
      you'd be it, i'd rather not
scuff up my coke whites
      under these tracks

Kennedy got jumped—bloody
      white t-shirt, blue jeans &
we took over the basketball
      court in our nikes

our voices acoustic now—no
      adolescent theory here. these shoes
get us into college digs—
      Harold & Kumar stomping
concrete holding backwoods & singing
      the right words to all

the wrong songs

                    on our way
back home.

now—

lust is falling asleep

      holding hands,

without understanding why

thrill is gone

there is a window. it
          is no metaphor for light
but grieves the sunset
          nonetheless.

i'm here to tell you how
          to escape loss without
breaking the glass.
          how to guard against

the frost of nightfall
          without sheathing
your skin. a small
          gesture or synonym

for love, you say. —listen,
          i cannot tell you how
to skin a fox, but i can
          show you the warmth

caught on the window-
          sill. i can place your
palm on my chest just
          before it beats. my chest

is no metaphor for loss
          of love. my love is no
metaphor for warmth.
          but listen, i can tell you

how to escape loss
          without breaking
the glass.

phototaxis

sweat of the delta, i'm writing
        this poem in dead summer.

skin thickset
        and sultry—

the fan oscillates, pushing
        warm air from one corner

to another. here, something is arresting
        about the heat, the way it girdles

each muscle movement into careful
        meditation. i ask you to dance

say, *play that song, you know—*
        the one we sung

with our entire bodies

        and reluctantly, you oblige. sway,
almost still,

        gnats held hostage,
phototaxis   positive.

nomenclature

i've forgotten what pain feels like, as if it belonged to me &

if you've ever owned anything, you understand my concern:

agony. ache. strain. struggle. torment. plague. pandemic. i am told:

if you have more than one name for a thing, you should let it go—

i toss the last of my death. dead. deceased. perish. pass, away—

what's another name for prey?

for Damion

i didn't know a poem
could write itself
                    until walking
Damion discovered
dead birds
on the sidewalk
& used them
as a simile,

            the ink splayed
across his notebook,

bird: like or as a body

dead:

a thing that doesn't have a name

                    for you

cayendo

i listen to "cayendo" & my chest sags.
weed makes everything new again,

                              this song's

chord progression,
          a small river in the backcountry somewhere
with only enough people in town for you, *Frank*—

i'm saying, few know the difference between falling
in love & self-preservation—
                                        you
somewhere, a still song
                    skipping along the surface
of the water
                    yes, i too know repeated violence

& its offspring   the gavel

                              drumming
                                    drumming—

footnotes for Kanye

after Jasmine Mans

1.

the first time i heard *pray for Kanye* was at a Black lives matter rally. not that prayer is antithetical, but prayer next to antiBlackness is a flood, not a life raft.

2.

as if there isn't a grandmother's last breath interceding for even the most defiant among us.

3.

there is something to be said about dying before death—how suffrage isn't always the antecedent, how some of us find glory in drowning.

4.

politics have taught me—your desires, Ye, no matter how deviant, don't outweigh your means & for that, i am afraid.

5.

i asked my mama about a world without the woman who birthed her whole at wauwatosa / she smiles & asks me to pass her the salt.

6.

i'm afraid cuz any day without a mother's smile is no day at all.

_____

7.

cuz if not god, my mama.

8.

if not a life raft, a flood.

9.

i'm afraid cuz you ain't talked to god in so long—

10.

Ye,   are you more brave than free? or more ignant than a
housefly missing the door?

11.

do you miss the door?

12.

when i listen to "no church in the wild," your voice is both the
mob & the non-believer.

_____

13.

are you still famous in your hood?

14.

because these kids still want to be you / they want to rap & make soul beats just like you / even though you just not you.

15.

tell me—   now, where' the south side?

Frank's opus: pink + orange

       well-oiled axis
don't break for breath.

       just keeps spinning
a map back to your name

       made before birth.
sings—101 south

       gently, without guardrails
as far as your wings flap

       Aunt Toni says: *surrender*
to air,   to fly

       & i've seemed to've
misplaced the audacity

       underneath these miles,
underneath all this pink-orange sky.

asking for a friend feat: Chris Abani & Danez Smith

listening to a podcast & Danez says americans are always inter-
ested in the *new* and Abani says language is how we know we exist
& Abani likens poetry to distilled beauty & i ~~interject silently and~~
ask why shouldn't we spend every day trying to be beautiful we've
been dying our whole life after all & Abani says he's like a bull in a
china shop trying to relearn elegance & i ~~interject~~ silently & Danez
says Abani thinks about poetry in terms of mathematics & so i ~~in-
terject~~ this time, mouth wide and ask how many reincarnations it
takes a Black body before it becomes beautiful or new—

**sitting in a wicker chair against
floral wallpaper in oakland heat**

there is a portrait of Huey Newton
     in my church.
it's communion sunday
and Mama has on her good shoes
with the gold links.
    the Jackson boys are dressed
to the nines
their pants starch-creased and hovering
    above their snakeskins like halos

Hueys in a Black beret—

but gone, *anyway*—

    what's blood without a body to show for it?

in the states, what is more righteous than a gun
    and a spear sitting
    at the left hand of god

on a wicker chair
    in oakland?

territory

i watch *into the cosmos* & feel

                              infinitely

small,

                  how the homies must
                     feel when they watch
                         the birth of a nation
                             or any other carbon-
               copy slave movie

no matter
how triumphant
the battle, the victor
is always
abundantly
white

                          i can't help but think
                          about the boys
                          i grew up with

who claimed to "run the city,"
not in colonial terms, but

                     as anatomy

how they've learned
        since birth
             to measure land, not
        by geography, but

through flesh & the taking of it

in this way, perhaps,
          the obsession has always been
the body
        & the destruction
                it's capable of wielding

or falling victim to

                      in this way, they too
                          seek something
new,

                              if not imaginative—

//

if not through
their hands,
then,
through
their bodies.

                in this way,
                    we are huge, after all

how the few feet
        separating our nikes
                does nothing
                    to render
                        the entire sky

between us.

how the quiet won't stop moving
long enough to be held

you borrow my chest
        because
the ocean is loud tonight
& nothing is more
        quiet
than a heartbeat

          until,
the tide is too much
          to corral
you stay
        for a while
ride the ripples
        to shore
& i figure
        this must be
what James Baldwin meant
        when he said
        love is irrational

how the quiet won't stop
        moving
long enough
        to be held

Frank's opus: solo

the bodies pile

jigsaw themselves

to memory somewhere //

somehow, you're solo

eyes red

& barely open

eyes cutting //

white & elusive

pupils // above

is-cape between fingers

a clysmic Osiris //

dancing & elusive

a misfiring bull //

      besieged

& somehow you're

so low // beneath

black & barely holy

love is the result of attempting to stay

here, death & love share a common ancestor:
recklessness   here, the mouth, a small auditorium
of things said while taking a last breath
or a single thing, a single mama
ricocheting off the pink of the mouth
her syllables within his uncontrol   a truth:
love is the result of attempting to stay
alive   here, death & love are two ineffable
creatures   here, a mama becomes a
gateway to god   here, if death, then, at least
while swallowing the name i love

bouquet

when we thought the world was ending, flowers began blooming
        —W. J. Lofton

if not a revolution, a broken window—
an angiosperm in my hand, a bouquet of flowers

in front of me, the shards glisten half yellow,
half opaque & arresting like a small child

under the arrest of something new, this is not
new, but i am preserved & anxious

all at once   the body always knows

how to signal pain, vivid colors
don't call me hero, i am no hero, i am

a white blood cell standing in front of this store,
smoking & amber, watching the spring bloom

no one told me the world was on fire

                    it's no secret

each day begins in darkness & ends dark

becomes golden for a little while
          in the middle

that is the bread i get on my knees for

             the sun's devices:

god—

                 & his hands

outstretched over the earth

             trying to keep warm

geography

after Tjawangwa Dema

in darvaza a fire has been burning since 1971

       since 1863
       since 1760
          1619
          1492
     since
     since
     since

someone's math was off

someone is still counting

in darvaza

drill

in america
drill and drill and drill

      no craters
      no air

the rig is buried above ground
the drill is Black

there is no oil
just fire
and drills made of porcelain

—someone is still counting

and fire
and fire
and fire

Frank's opus: skyline to

got my metal
on.
didn't know my body before
you &
today, more than yesterday
& the day before
slips—

      quests itself.
anchored
to january
how it never seems to
commemorate
new shit like
we do

no matter how many shots
we take
we always wake up
cold as

december
with brand-new headaches.

Baldwin discovers pepsi on sale

come,

i hear the world is to die for.

**sitting in a wicker chair against
floral wallpaper in oakland heat**

wicker chair out front since before cointelpro
            bludgeoned the panthers.

we've come because it's easter
                            and we're hungry. inside,

Marvin Gaye's falsetto

                seeps in like a gentle flood

                    and the kitchen becomes
                    a small soul train line
                    for 12 minutes instead.

all these bodies bending like prayer.

                Black means religion is second

only to dancing.

how to spell redemption

       what i figure craziest about each lynching
is not the blood, but the pentecost

       that fills the body. coxing death
to death, resurrecting the spirit.

       Mama always bought a size and a half
too big, so they'd last. & filled

       the gap with plenty of prayer to order
my steps. maybe in a similar way

       they want us to grow into our coffins too—
maybe we're supposed to learn

       how to spell by scribbling redemption inside
the casket walls with our fingernails.

maybe redemption will come
       in due time. or in just enough time

for a ripe body to emerge,
       with enough holy to kickstart a revolution.

interloping

i first think of my brother's verbs,

          how each of them moves

in ways frowned upon

       he mentions life

as an action

& allows all the blood

       to flow from his heart

to his head

     as if hanging

upside down

while the smallest of us

              watch him

glide above, devilishly angelic—

i think of his tongue   swinging—

   his righteous rebellion   swinging

his voice, an interloping wish   —swinging—

        back &

forth.

Frank's opus: self-control

the bridge floors me
each time i collect enough

courage to play it all
the way through.

this anxiety
wants to forget—hold

on to almost white
morning sun slit through

canyon live oak.
we crash at dawn

fall in love
backwards

as if tomorrow was
an uninvited third wheel.

it is more glorious this way
the sun searching for us & all

your shadow
a kestrel flying in place

your body, already leaving.

you tilt your head
toward me to say

nothing gold can stay

          & yet here we are
          again,   dancing

as if music is the shadow

          of a figure just out of sight
          you are not near,

but this song is. again.

chile' as in you

                  it gotta be important—
how she begins every sentence.

      i'm wide-eyed as a six-year-old waiting
for instructions
that don't come in steps, but vignettes separated
by long breaths. says *chile'*—& i shrink
to listen

makes me
      forget who i belong to. a boy. a man.

a prayer in each inaudible sound—

                  says   *chile'*,

& i'm a congregation,

even the parts of me that've sinned

too much to belong to god.

she explains the best way to cure a common cough
while stirring a pot of spaghetti large enough

to feed a family
that does not live here,

but we're grateful nonetheless—

salvation

as a kid, my sisters shared
only difference. now,
each of them closely
resembles my mother.
the oldest looks at me

with her eyes and smiles
with them too. before a chide,
a decompressed chest
as if releasing the scold
from her body unhurried,

she, a hospice,
says my name,
& i listen most.

i am a boy again & don't mind
at all. in this way, i can press
in & drop my guard while
she tells me, it gets easier.
somehow,

i believe her. somehow,
my mother's eyes, a sort
of lifeline or sedation. either
way, a tender gaze in concert,
smiles the smile that leaves

you bare bottom & broken,
the way a sinner feels
after confessing sin,
except in this box,

there is no sin.
only salvation.

nobody loves me but my mother
& she could be jivin' too

after all these years, i figure,
love doesn't flee, we do, somehow
in this stitched dream, forget

there are rocks older
than our grandmother's great
grandmother & her grandmother's

too. believed that love somehow ebbed or
flowed & i'm convinced nobody truly
knows how old the earth really is

or if love is older—

Frank's opus: nights

bring   the boy's

      wild-   fire

tell him   it's enough

    to reach   expired

warmth   to spark

   a small   tryst or

séance or   secret.

//

bring   the breath

   a psalm   a poem

it knows   it cannot

                hold in

its mouth   like

   a tongue   spitting fire

curling into   itself.

language for exhaustion

inter-garrison
passing
nix & life
my foot off the gas

i'm neutral

for a half mile
before
my driveway i spool
to a stop.

that is my language
for exhaustion

space and time.

my grandfather too
spoke.

slurred—

wrapping cars
around telephone poles

each night

after work.

belching

I didn't mean that, Mamma.
I know you fed us and all.
I was talkin' 'bout something else.
Like. Like. Playin' with us.
Did you ever, you know,
play with us?
                    —Toni Morrison, *Sula*

sorry for all my peering
off
had to make sure
the coast was clear
enough for you to jump
off
the ledge
head first, *anyway*

as i was saying—
if you've ever had to push
your belch out
you know what it feels like
to have laughter
caught in your throat

Frank's opus: solo (reprise) erasure

                       no more

     geronimo!

    i

        admit

     that another shot
ain't an event

so low that no more

of you, and

i

know what it's like

insensitive

but my halo

     way low, it feels like it's bent

feel like a kid

lookin'
with astonishment

watchin' the *close* to an end

after 20 years in,

i'm so naïve

i was under

      i've stumbled

was i working just way too hard?

considering the defense production act

the defense production act gives the president several
powers to ensure that supplies for national defense are produced
by u.s. industries and distributed to places that need them.
        —the washington post

before bed, i tell my daughter i love her for the 11th time
today & her mouth yields: *Daddy, you're a builder!*

i take inventory of the day, reckoning the bookshelf i built
next to her bed, holding each nail near the head. i consider
my grandfather, his unfailing advice, and swing
from the elbow once more, like he taught me—

i haven't felt the effects of the defense production act except
through my grandmother-in-law's hands & all the other
grandmother hands that still have breath. how they've stopped
manufacturing prayers briefly to manufacture

face masks, how   in some cultures, mouths don't
mouth i love you. i think   how we are made holy
not by our hearts, but through our hands. i press my lips
together, take my fingers to her cheek, as if to say—

in defense of survival

why should Black people be such survivors all the time?
        —Chen Chen (tweet)

I don't know but it's better
than not having nothing to fight for
        —a person's response (tweet)

                        again, my niggas die &
they label those of us on deck
"survivors," in the longest stretch of the word
        as in, we entered this world dying
& count our blessings each time god takes
                        our friends instead

pardon my audacity,

                        not even small prey
desire to survive

**sitting in a wicker chair against
floral wallpaper in oakland heat**

the day america stormed
        america
i was Black and in exile
        for yanking a tulip
from the ground

                i shouldn't have,
but wanted something
        more beautiful to die
before i did—

call it civil disobedience

Frank's opus: godspeed

fault lines are stronger than any faith
i've ever mustered. there are mountains,

i do not move. & this isn't a mountain
so much as it is a hill. & this kind of love isn't

movement so much as it's biblical destruction
perhaps: our prayers are too many & god is too

few to collect them all. perhaps, an aftershock
is the earth's invocation for less movement.

i know my voice is no match for an earthquake
but the premise of prayer is not to watch the sky

open, but to feel the ground shake beneath
my feet without asking. prayer is not asking,

prayer is not about asking. prayer is a
tremor we don't have a grand enough name for.

mausoleum of flowers

split earth's rotting wound. your body,
a mausoleum hanging over its lip—
like a made thing. plucking flowers

on our walks, you study them close,
stumbling over your brand-new feet.
they'll die before we make it home,

i don't say. you are a botanist
& know all about self-
preservation. know there is no grey

in death—& you are very much alive

NOTES

poems "cayendo," "Frank's opus: godspeed," "Frank's opus: nights," "Frank's opus: nikes," "Frank's opus: pink + orange," "Frank's opus: self-control," "Frank's opus: skyline to," "Frank's opus: solo," and "Frank's opus: solo (reprise) erasure" reference songs from Frank Ocean's album *Blond*.

"wading" includes a line inspired by the title of Cassandra Clare's book *City of Glass*.

"fear" includes a passage from Proverbs 23:13 and a line from Kendrick Lamar.

"Frank's opus: poolside convo erasure" is an erasure poem of Frank Ocean's post to Tumblr as reported and printed in the following article: Yoo, Noah. "Frank Ocean Shares Notes about the Making of *Blond* and *Boys Don't Cry* Magazine." *Pitchfork.* August 20, 2016, https://pitchfork.com/news/67685-frank -ocean-shares-notes-about-the-making-of-blond-and-boy s-dont-cry-magazine/?mbid=social_twitter.

"footnotes for Kanye" uses lyrics from Kanye West's "Home," "No Church in the Wild," and "Glory."

"asking for a friend feat: Chris Abani & Danez Smith" includes quotes or paraphrases from *VS Podcast*.

"sitting in a wicker chair against floral wallpaper in oakland heat" is a title inspired by a line in Eddie S. Glaude Jr.'s book, *Begin Again*.

"how the quiet won't stop moving long enough to be held" includes a quote from James Baldwin from "Full Conversation with James Baldwin and Nikki Giovanni in London, 1971." SOUL! https://www.youtube.com/watch?v=KL_cM7SXfbo&t=3221s.

"Frank's opus: self-control" includes the title of a poem by Robert Frost.

"nobody loves me but my mother (& she could be jivin' too)" is a title after B. B. King.

"Frank's opus: solo (reprise) erasure" is an erasure poem with lyrics from "Solo (Reprise)" by Frank Ocean and André 3000.

"considering the defense production act" uses an epigraph from the following article: Rizzo, Salvador. "What to Know about the Defense Production Act." *Washington Post*. March 25, 2020. https://www.washingtonpost.com/politics/2020/03/25/is-trump-using-defense-production-act/.

ACKNOWLEDGMENTS

immense gratitude to the following presses, publications, and websites where poems from this collection originally appeared:

Columbia Journal: "mama"
Flypaper: "bouquet," "in defense of survival"
Obsidian: "chile' as in you," "fear," "footnotes for Kanye," "on deciding to leave my tail out," "sunday in oakland"
Rust + Moth: "do not gather flowers for me"

the book epigraph is from "Malcolm" by Sonia Sanchez in *Shake Loose My Skin: New and Selected Poems*, published by Beacon Press. reprinted by permission of the author.

this book wouldn't be possible without the stories told by late grandfather, Bernard Clemons, as well as my mother, Sandra Garrett, and sister, Tenesha Smith. i love you beyond measurement and understanding.

much gratitude to all of my family and friends for your unfailing and unstained love, even as you have no knowledge of line break or syntax. your stories are grander than any element of craft could ever be.

to Quintin Collins, i couldn't ask for a better literary sibling. for your encouragement and feedback, i am indebted.

sincerest of love to the homies for their creative sustenance and for keeping me at any point during the writing of this book: Michael McGee Jr., Douglas Barron, Jamel Freeman, Daniella Toosie-Watson, Crystal Todoroff.

to mentors, past and present: Iain Haley Pollock, Laure-Anne Bosselaar, Nicole Terez Dutton, Kathleen Aguero, Dzvinia Orlowski, and the whole Solstice MFA program family, where many of the ideas for these poems were birthed—thank you.

much love to the Abolition and Decolonial Education Collective at California State University, Monterey Bay for being my small family of support and inspiration.

to my most essential family: Quianna, thank you for your love and steadfastness when all else fails. lastly, to my Poet Genesis, whom this book wouldn't exist without. this collection is for you, little one. you are the flowers here. bloom.

CAVANKERRY'S MISSION

A not-for-profit literary press serving art and community, CavanKerry is committed to expanding the reach of poetry and other fine literature to a general readership by publishing works that explore the emotional and psychological landscapes of everyday life, and to bringing that art to the underserved where they live, work, and receive services.

OTHER BOOKS IN THE EMERGING VOICES SERIES

My Painted Warriors, Peggy Penn
Neighborhood Register, Marcus Jackson
Night Sessions, David S. Cho
Underlife, January Gill O'Neil
The Second Night of the Spirit, Bhisham Bherwani
The Red Canoe: Love In Its Making, Joan Cusack Handler
WE AREN'T WHO WE ARE and this world isn't either,
   Christine Korfhage
Imago, Joseph O. Legaspi
Through a Gate of Trees, Susan Jackson
Against Which, Ross Gay
The Silence of Men, Richard Jeffrey Newman
The Disheveled Bed, Andrea Carter Brown
The Fork Without Hunger, Laurie Lamon
The Singers I Prefer, Christian Barter
Momentum, Catherine Doty
An Imperfect Lover, Georgianna Orsini
Soft Box, Celia Bland
Rattle, Eloise Bruce
Eye Level: Fifty Histories, Christopher Matthews
GlOrious, Joan Cusack Handler
The Palace of Ashes, Sherry Fairchok
Silk Elegy, Sondra Gash
So Close, Peggy Penn
Kazimierz Square, Karen Chase
A Day This Lit, Howard Levy

This book was printed on paper from responsible sources.

Mausoleum of Flowers has been set in New Atten, a sans-serif typeface intended to achieve a noticeable charm and a personable tone while still preserving the integrity of the text. It was designed by Miles Newlyn of Newlyn Type Foundry.